Becoming Visible

How Black Men Navigate, Resist, and Transform Teacher Education

---

Dr. William A. Anders

ENLA Solutions Group, LLC

Becoming Visible: How Black Men Navigate, Resist, and Transform Teacher Education

Updated Edition – May 2026

Published by ENLA Solutions Group, LLC

This book is based on research and lived experiences within teacher education. Identifying details have been changed to protect confidentiality.

First published 2026. Printed in the United States of America.

For every Black man who entered the room questioning whether he belonged—

and stayed anyway.

Contents

PREFACE

Why This Book Exists

This book was not born from theory.

It was born from lived experience—mine, and that of Black men I encountered across higher education as they entered, navigated, and at times struggled within teacher education systems not designed with them in mind.

Patterns began to emerge. Men who entered with clarity of purpose began to question themselves after a single comment. Talent that arrived with confidence left conversations uncertain. What was visible in those moments was not a lack of ability. It was a misalignment in recognition.

Confidence was reframed as attitude. Critical thinking became resistance. Cultural knowledge was treated as perspective rather than expertise. Leadership potential was narrowed into assumptions about behavior rather than expanded as intellectual capacity.

That clarity deepened through my own advanced study. What I had observed from the outside began surfacing in my own experience. I recognized familiar dynamics in new contexts. I understood, from the inside, what it means to be visible yet not fully understood. Included yet not fully centered.

I observed institutions articulating diversity commitments while sustaining daily practices that quietly undermined them. I learned what it means to be affirmed in principle but unsupported in practice.

That shift sharpened everything.

This book is not simply an analysis. It is a research-informed account grounded in lived reality. It refuses to allow Black men's experiences to be minimized, misdefined, or rendered invisible. It centers them fully—honoring their intellectual, emotional, and cultural contributions while recognizing them as knowledge producers in their own right.

This book speaks to multiple audiences. To Black men navigating these systems: it is a mirror that names what you have experienced and a map that orients what comes next. To faculty and administrators: it is an account of what your decisions produce. Not to generate defensiveness—to create clarity. To researchers and policymakers: it is data and argument, grounded in experience and connected to structural analysis.

Black men deserve more than survival in teacher education. They deserve belonging, affirmation, and structural support aligned with the brilliance they bring.

Too often, Black men appear in teacher education literature as data points, case studies, or recruitment priorities. Their perspectives are engaged only when race becomes a moment of focus. This work centers them fully.

It honors their intellectual, emotional, and cultural contributions. It positions them as knowledge producers and theorists in their own right. Not as the subjects of a study. As the architects of insight that the field has too long overlooked.

This is where the work begins.

INTRODUCTION

What This Book Is For

This book is not an argument about whether Black men belong in teacher education.

That question, though often implied, is not the one that requires examination. The more pressing inquiry is this: what happens when Black men enter systems not designed with them in mind and are expected to succeed within them?

That is the territory this book explores. How institutional structures shape experience. How those experiences, in turn, reveal the limits of existing design. How what appears personal is almost always patterned.

At the center of this analysis is one critical distinction: what looks interpersonal often reflects something structural. That moves the conversation away from individual shortcomings and toward the systems that produce them. Persistence, belonging, and success become matters of institutional design—not individual disposition.

For Black men in teacher education, this matters in a very specific way. They are not only learning how to teach. They are learning how to move within systems where their presence is both visible and frequently misunderstood. They interpret expectations while managing perception. They engage feedback while assessing its clarity. They demonstrate competence within structures that don't always communicate how competence is defined.

This book does not argue that teacher education is beyond repair. Quite the opposite.

It argues that teacher education has more capacity for transformation than it has chosen to use—and that the experiences of Black men are among the clearest guides available for what that transformation requires.

How to Read This Book

Each chapter moves across three layers. First, lived experience—real moments inside classrooms, advising sessions, and field placements. Second, structural insight—analysis that connects those moments to institutional design. Third, strategic response—concrete Playbook Moves you can apply immediately.

The C.A.R.E. Model—Community, Access, Representation, and Equity—runs through everything. It is introduced fully in Chapter 12. Every chapter before it builds the case. Every chapter after it applies the frame.

Who This Book Is For

Black male high school students considering teaching. College students navigating entry into teacher education. Black men already in programs trying to make sense of what they are experiencing. And educators and institutions seeking to understand and respond—structurally, not symbolically.

Every section is designed to move the reader toward one of three recognitions: This is not just me—this is the system. Now I know how to move. I can see myself in this work, and I'm ready for it.

Awareness alone does not produce transformation. Insight must lead to action. This book is designed to be used—as a mirror to recognize patterns, a lens to examine systems, and a framework to guide change.

Teacher education operates through both explicit instruction and implicit expectation. Coursework, field placements, and certification requirements are clearly defined. But many of the norms governing success remain unspoken. How professionalism is interpreted. How authority is expressed. How feedback is delivered. How evaluation is conducted.

For those already familiar with those norms, navigation feels intuitive. For others, it requires continuous interpretation. For Black men, it requires both—while also managing how their presence is perceived in real time.

That is not a personal challenge. It is a structural one. And this book names it as such.

CHAPTER 1

Do We Even Belong Here?

Something happens the first time a Black man looks around the room in a teacher education program and recognizes that the absence is not incidental.

It is architectural.

Not just at the table. Not just in his cohort. Across the faculty, the curriculum, the leadership—the design itself signals who was expected and who was accommodated.

The question that surfaces is not about capability. Preparation is not in doubt. The question is structural: Were these spaces built with Black men in mind as intellectual contributors? Or built for someone else, with room made available later?

> **Visibility does not guarantee clarity. Being seen does not ensure being understood.**

WHAT TO EXPECT IN THIS CHAPTER

This chapter examines the first disorienting recognition many Black men face in teacher education: the space was not designed with them at its center.

It explores how that recognition surfaces, what it costs to carry, and how to interpret it as structural rather than personal. By the end, you will have language for what this experience actually is—and a clearer sense of what is producing it.

WHAT ENTRY ACTUALLY LOOKS LIKE

Access is often framed as the primary barrier. For many Black men, it is only the beginning.

They arrive with purpose. They engage coursework, participate in discussions, move through field experiences with intention. Then, gradually, the challenge shifts. It stops being about mastering content and starts being about interpreting the conditions under which that content is evaluated.

A response in class draws different scrutiny. Written feedback identifies a concern without pointing toward a solution. An evaluation references a standard that was never fully explained. Each moment alone may feel minor. Together, they shape how the environment is understood.

Over time, these men recognize something important: demonstrating competence is not always enough. They must also understand how competence is defined within the space. That is a different and harder task.

> **REAL TALK**
>
> Here's what nobody tells you going in: you're not just learning how to teach. You're learning how teaching is evaluated—and those are not always the same thing. The second skill is rarely in any syllabus. You have to learn it by paying close attention to patterns most people around you don't notice.

THE HIDDEN CURRICULUM OF NAVIGATION

Teacher education runs on two simultaneous tracks.

The first is explicit: coursework, field placements, certification requirements. The second is implicit: norms about how to communicate, how to project authority, how to receive criticism, how to be legible within the space.

For those already familiar with those norms, navigation feels intuitive. The unspoken rules were part of their upbringing. For others, those rules must be learned in real time—through repeated exposure, trial, and calibration.

Black men in these spaces are often navigating both tracks at once. They are learning how to teach while learning how their teaching will be interpreted. That doubled awareness is exhausting in ways that rarely get acknowledged.

This is not simply adjustment. It is strategic adaptation.

And it is costly. Every interaction that requires pre-calculation. Every piece of written communication revised for strategic effect. Every decision about how much of yourself to bring into a room. These are not frictionless exchanges. They are investments of attention, energy, and emotional bandwidth.

This cost is not distributed equally across teacher education candidates. It falls most heavily on those whose identity is most likely to be misread, most likely to produce institutional friction. When this cost is invisible to the institution—when evaluation frameworks don't account for it—it functions as a structural disadvantage operating alongside other, more visible forms of inequity.

SCENARIO: FIRST OBSERVATION FEEDBACK

A candidate teaches a strong lesson. Standards are met, students are engaged, pacing is intentional. The supervisor's written feedback opens with two positives, then pivots to composure and classroom presence. Nothing about instructional design. Nothing about the questions he chose or the scaffolding he built. Just presence. He leaves wondering: Was the lesson good, or was I just manageable?

THE DEEPER PATTERN

These dynamics don't begin in higher education. They build across years.

From early academic development forward, Black men develop an awareness of how they are read within academic spaces—how attention is distributed, how expectations are communicated, what gets amplified and what gets ignored. By the time they enter teacher education, that awareness is already calibrated.

Higher education doesn't erase those earlier experiences. It reframes them. Teacher preparation environments present themselves as reflective and inclusive. Yet beneath that framing are implicit norms that shape how participation is recognized and evaluated. For some, participation feels seamless. For others, it requires continuous interpretation.

Entry is possible. Recognition is uneven. Belonging is conditional.

The presence of Black men in teacher education does not call belonging into question. It reveals a question of design. Until that question is addressed, participation will continue to require interpretation and belonging will remain incomplete.

That is not an individual limitation. It is a structural one.

There is a particular kind of professionalism that is rarely discussed in teacher education: the professionalism of remaining intact while being systematically misread. Not the professionalism defined in rubrics. The professionalism of continuing to show up with intellectual seriousness and emotional steadiness in an environment that has not fully made space for you.

Black men practice this continuously. It deserves to be named, recognized, and ultimately relieved—not celebrated as an expectation.

What teacher education hasn't fully reckoned with is this: the experience of Black men in these programs is not primarily a story about individual struggle. It is a story about institutional design. About who the system was built for and who it requires more from.

When expectations remain unspoken, some candidates can read the room intuitively. Others must learn the room through trial, observation, and calibration. The difference in effort required is not a measure of ability. It is a measure of familiarity with norms that were never designed to be universal.

That gap has consequences. It shapes how Black men experience feedback, interpret evaluation, and position themselves within programs. It influences how much energy is available for the intellectual work of becoming a teacher—because so much has already been spent on navigation.

This book is not asking teacher education to lower its standards. It is asking it to examine whose experiences those standards were built around. And to design systems where belonging does not require continuous interpretation.

In Chapter 12, we'll name exactly what that redesign requires. The C.A.R.E. Model—Community, Access, Representation, Equity—gives it structure. For now, hold this: every pattern described in this chapter is a design problem. And design problems have design solutions.

The work ahead is not for those who struggle. It is for those who built something despite the struggle.

PLAYBOOK MOVE

- Map the room early. Identify who holds formal authority and who holds informal influence. They are not always the same person.
- Name the implicit norms in writing. When you observe an expectation never stated aloud, document it. This reduces the cognitive load of rediscovering it later.
- Distinguish between feedback on performance and feedback on perception. Both matter—but they require different responses.
- Document your navigation: what you observed, what you adjusted, and what it cost. That record is both personal protection and institutional evidence.

CHAPTER 2

The Historical Weight We Carry

Black men do not enter teacher education as blank slates.

They arrive with history. Not as a burden—but as context. Long before coursework begins, there is an accumulated understanding of who has been permitted to learn in this country, who has been permitted to teach, and what it has historically cost Black people to claim authority in educational spaces.

That history doesn't stay outside institutional walls. It comes in with you.

> **Entry into teacher preparation is not a neutral starting point. It is an arrival into a system already shaped by expectation.**

What to Expect in This Chapter

This chapter traces what was built by Black educators before formal certification systems existed, what was dismantled during desegregation, and how those patterns continue to structure teacher education today.

Understanding this history is not optional background. It is essential context for interpreting what happens in these programs now.

What Was Built—and What Was Dismantled

There was a time when educating Black people in this country was illegal.

Literacy was criminalized. To learn to read was to challenge control. To teach was to disrupt power. And yet Black communities didn't abandon education. They redefined it.

Learning took place in churches, in homes, passed quietly from one person to another. Education was not separate from survival. It was a strategy for it. After Emancipation, that commitment intensified. Black educators served as translators between communities and systems designed to exclude—teaching not just academic content but political literacy, economic awareness, and civic preparation.

Black men entering teacher education today are not newcomers to this field.

They are part of a tradition that existed long before formal certification pathways were created.

> **REAL TALK**
>
> Here's what the history books often skip: desegregation didn't just open doors for Black students. It closed a lot of doors for Black educators. Hundreds of Black teachers and principals—people who had built schools that worked, that communities trusted—were displaced when integration happened. White institutions absorbed the students but not the leadership. That erasure has never been fully repaired. You are navigating a system shaped by that history right now.

How the Past Shapes the Present

Teaching remains a predominantly white profession. Within many programs, Black men complete their entire preparation without encountering a single faculty member who shares their racial and gender identity.

That absence carries weight. It shapes how authority is modeled, how mentorship is accessed, and how professional futures are imagined.

What gets presented as professionalism is not neutral. Communication styles, emotional expression, approaches to authority—these were shaped by dominant cultural norms that were never identified as such. They were just presented as the standard. When Black men bring different forms of knowledge and expression, institutions often require alignment with existing norms rather than expanding to incorporate new ones.

Confidence gets read as aggression. Directness becomes defiance. Cultural knowledge gets dismissed as mere perspective.

These are not random misreadings. They follow a pattern. And that pattern has a history.

Black men are not entering systems that are broken. They are entering systems that remain incomplete.

When you know the history, you interpret your present experience more accurately. You stop internalizing structural misalignment as personal failure. You understand that what you carry—knowledge of community, of how learning functions in real environments, of what young people need to see in order to believe in their own potential—is not supplemental. It is foundational. It always has been.

The absence of institutional acknowledgment is itself a structural pattern worth naming. When programs don't teach the history of Black educators alongside the history of education itself, they communicate something about whose experience constitutes the field's foundation.

When you understand where you come from within the arc of this profession, the daily friction of institutional navigation takes on different meaning. Misrecognition becomes less personal. The purpose becomes more durable.

The lineage of Black educators in this country is long. It is distinguished. And it is largely uncelebrated within the institutional spaces that now ask Black men to earn credentials before they can teach. That tension is worth naming.

SCENARIO: THE ADVISOR WHO DIDN'T KNOW

During his second semester, a candidate asked his advisor to recommend scholarship on Black male educators in the K–12 pipeline. The advisor paused, then suggested some general diversity literature. Not a single title by a Black scholar. Not a single piece on the specific tradition he was entering. The candidate went home and found the scholarship himself. It took him forty-five minutes. Forty-five minutes to locate a century-long tradition of Black educators, researchers, and theorists whose work directly addressed what he was navigating. The program hadn't assigned a single piece of it.

PLAYBOOK MOVE

- Study the history of Black educators in your region. Know who was displaced, who built schools, who was recognized and who wasn't. That context will ground you when current dynamics feel disorienting.
- When you notice misrecognition—confidence read as aggression, clarity read as defiance—pause before internalizing it. Ask: Is this about me, or is this a pattern with a longer history?
- Seek out scholarship by Black educators and historians of education. Their frameworks will give you language for what you are experiencing.
- Connect with Black educators who have been in the field for ten or more years. Their retrospective view of what helped is one of the most direct forms of institutional intelligence available.

CHAPTER 3

Pathways Into Teaching: No Straight Lines, Just Purpose

Teacher education is built around an assumption: that the path into teaching is linear.

Early interest. Declared major. Coursework. Student teaching. Classroom.

Clean. Predictable. Expected.

For most Black men, that path does not exist. And the systems designed around it were not built with their realities in mind.

Their pathways are not unclear. They are unrecognized.

WHAT TO EXPECT IN THIS CHAPTER

This chapter examines how Black men actually enter teaching—the non-linear, community-rooted, purpose-driven journeys that institutions frequently misread as delay or inconsistency. By the end, you will have language for articulating your own pathway with confidence.

WHERE TEACHING ACTUALLY BEGINS

For most Black men, teaching starts long before any program.

A student keeps coming back with questions. A teammate responds to coaching in a way that surprises both of you. A kid in the neighborhood starts looking to you—and you feel the weight of that responsibility.

Institutions don't create this teacher. The community already recognizes him. Black men are often already teaching before they ever call it that—mentoring in after-school programs, coaching teams, leading youth groups, tutoring peers.

These experiences build the exact capacities teacher education programs claim to value: relational intelligence, cultural fluency, patience under pressure. They just don't come with a credential attached.

SCENARIO: THE NON-TRADITIONAL ENTRY

Marcus spent three years in youth development before pursuing his certification. When he met with a program advisor, the first question was about the gap on his transcript. Not about what he had learned leading a program of forty students. Not about the curriculum he had designed. About the gap. He left that meeting wondering whether the institution was interested in what he had to offer—or only in what he had missed.

He knew what he had built. Forty students. A weekly curriculum he designed himself. A space where kids came back because they chose to. He had watched students develop confidence he could actually see—the way they started sitting up straighter, asking questions, holding eye contact.

None of that appeared in the question the advisor asked.

He didn't leave that meeting angry. He left it quieter than he had arrived. And that quiet said something about the gap between what he carried and what the program was prepared to see.

WHAT GETS MISREAD AS DELAY

Teacher education programs are structured around a narrow model of the ideal candidate.

Direct entry from high school. Early commitment to an education major. Uninterrupted enrollment. Smooth transition into student teaching.

Most Black men navigating this path are also managing financial responsibilities, family commitments, and work obligations. What looks like delay from the outside is often disciplined navigation under pressure.

Gaps get questioned. Changes in direction get scrutinized. What is often missed is the context behind those decisions. What appears irregular is, in reality, navigation. What looks like delay is often persistence.

Black men are not late to teaching. They are arriving through pathways shaped by both purpose and responsibility.

> **REAL TALK**
>
> Stop apologizing for your path. The men who came to teaching through youth work, military service, a career change, or years of community involvement often have more real-world instructional experience than candidates who went straight through. The issue is not what you have. It's whether the institution knows how to recognize it. That is their limitation, not yours.

PURPOSE AS THE THROUGH LINE

What connects these non-linear journeys is not a shared timeline. It is a shared direction.

Something continues to pull these men toward the work. A sense of responsibility to students who will see themselves in you. To communities that shaped you. To the lineage of educators who built pathways without formal recognition.

That purpose is not soft. It is durable. It sustains people through programs that weren't built for them and into classrooms where their presence changes something.

Teacher education does not lack pathways. It fails to recognize the ones that already exist.

And the men who arrive through those unrecognized pathways often bring something programs struggle to produce through formal instruction: a genuine relationship to the communities they will serve. That relationship is not incidental. It is the foundation of culturally responsive teaching.

This book is not asking programs to lower standards. It is asking them to expand what they measure—to include the full scope of what effective teaching requires. Relational intelligence. Cultural fluency. Community knowledge. The ability to meet learners where they are.

Some programs have already started. They build explicit processes for recognizing prior learning, train advisors to read non-linear pathways as assets, and create space for candidates to document what they already know. The results are measurably different.

Until that expansion happens broadly, the burden falls on candidates to translate their experience into language the institution can hear. That translation should not be necessary. But it is. Knowing how to do it is itself a form of preparation.

Name your experience precisely. Connect it to the competencies programs claim to value. Make the case not defensively, but with the confidence of someone who understands that the institution's frameworks are incomplete—not that your experience is insufficient.

PLAYBOOK MOVE

- Frame your non-linear path as an asset, not a liability. Lead with what you learned, not what you missed.
- Document your informal teaching experience concretely. Youth development, coaching, tutoring—quantify it, name the skills it built, describe the outcomes. Make it legible on paper.
- Identify advisors and faculty who understand non-traditional pathways. Find the ones who see your experience accurately.
- Connect your reason for entering teaching to your professional statement and portfolio. Purpose is your most durable professional asset.
- When program timelines create pressure around pace, ask your advisor to walk you through the full sequence and identify any flexibility. Some constraints are real; others are presented as fixed when they are not.

CHAPTER 4

Representation and Identity: Teaching While Black and Male

There is a particular kind of silence that follows Black men into teacher education spaces.

It is not empty. It is structured. It carries expectation, projection, and interpretation before any introduction takes place. Before a word is spoken, assumptions begin to form. Presence is acknowledged—but not always engaged.

> ***Black men often live within a dual condition—immediately visible, and simultaneously under-recognized.***

WHAT TO EXPECT IN THIS CHAPTER

This chapter examines how representation operates in practice rather than in policy.

It explores the dual condition Black men navigate—visible and under-recognized simultaneously—and how intellectual authority is distributed unevenly across institutional spaces. It also examines the real impact Black male educators have in classrooms, and why that impact is worth staying for.

THE DOUBLE CONDITION

Their bodies are noticed before their ideas are explored. Their presence is acknowledged before their scholarship is considered.

Visibility does not guarantee recognition. It often precedes misinterpretation.

This is what W.E.B. Du Bois named double consciousness—seeing yourself through your own understanding while simultaneously tracking how you are perceived through a racialized lens. In teacher education, that awareness becomes professionalized. Black men are not only engaging with content. They are managing how that engagement will be read.

When class conversations turn toward race or equity, something in the room shifts. Attention redirects. The expectation to contribute becomes implied. Presence becomes synonymous with perspective. Black men are positioned as representatives before being recognized as scholars.

Their contributions are affirmed. But the affirmation reveals the pattern: insight is received as personal experience rather than theoretical contribution.

SCENARIO: THE RACE DISCUSSION

A class conversation turns to equity in K–12 education. The room shifts—a subtle reorientation toward the two Black men in the cohort. No one says anything directly. But the expectation is in the air. One of them offers a comment grounded in theory and experience. It is acknowledged warmly—as personal narrative. The theoretical dimension goes unaddressed. The discussion moves on.

WHEN REPRESENTATION GETS REDUCED TO SYMBOL

Intellectual authority circulates unevenly in these spaces.

Identity becomes the primary lens through which participation is invited. Broader scholarly engagement gets constrained. In collaborative work, contributions may be overlooked. In academic discussions, engagement may narrow once topics move beyond race and identity.

When the intellectual contributions of Black male educators are consistently filtered through a lens of identity rather than engaged on their analytical merits, the field loses something consequential. It loses the theoretical perspective that comes from navigating multiple social positions simultaneously. It loses the pedagogical insight that emerges from deep community knowledge.

When intellectual authority is expanded, representation deepens. When identity is reduced to symbolic inclusion, representation narrows.

> REAL TALK
>
> There is a difference between being engaged as a participant and being relied upon as a representative. One expands your intellectual authority. The other constrains it. Learn to feel the difference in the room. It will inform how you position your contributions.

WHAT ACTUAL IMPACT LOOKS LIKE

Despite these conditions, the impact Black men have in educational spaces is measurable and significant.

Classrooms shift when authority is expressed through care, intellectual engagement, and cultural understanding. For many students—particularly those who have never seen a Black man in a nurturing intellectual role—that presence is formative. It reshapes what they believe teaching can look like. It expands what they believe they can become.

SCENARIO: WHAT SHE SAID AFTER CLASS

At the end of a unit on argument and evidence, a seventh-grader stayed behind. She stood at the door for a moment, then turned back. "You're the first teacher who argued with me like I was right," she said. She didn't mean the teacher agreed with her. She meant he had engaged her thinking seriously enough to push back. She had never experienced that before. He had been teaching for four months.

That is the version of representation worth building toward. Not visibility in recruitment materials. Presence with authority in the spaces that shape the profession.

Becoming visible, in this fullest sense, requires that institutions change the conditions that determine who gets recognized and what that recognition makes possible.

CHAPTER 5

Belonging and the Architecture of Isolation

Belonging is one of the most widely used words in education.

It appears in mission statements, strategic plans, and student success frameworks. It is rarely defined with precision. And it is almost never examined as a structural condition.

Too often, belonging is treated as a feeling that either emerges or doesn't. What gets missed is that belonging is built. It is designed. And in most teacher education programs, it was designed with someone else in mind.

> *Academic success does not resolve structural isolation.*

THE DIFFERENCE BETWEEN SUPPORT AND BELONGING

Institutions often conflate these two things. They are not the same.

Support addresses barriers. Belonging affirms identity. It signals that one's presence was expected here.

A student can meet every academic requirement, perform well in coursework, receive positive evaluations—and still experience a persistent sense of disconnection from the environment shaping his professional identity. That disconnection is not about performance. It is about recognition. And recognition is structural.

SCENARIO: THE HIGH PERFORMER WHO STILL FEELS PERIPHERAL

Darius has a 3.8 GPA. His supervisors consistently rate him highly. Faculty describe him as one of the strongest candidates in his cohort. He also cannot name a single faculty member who has asked him about his long-term goals. He has never seen a Black man teach a course in his program. He attends every professional development session and leaves each one feeling slightly more invisible. His academic record says he belongs. His daily experience says something different.

After one of those sessions, he sat in his car for a few minutes before driving home. Not processing anything complicated. Just sitting with the feeling. The kind of tired that doesn't come from working hard. The kind that comes from being somewhere and still feeling like you're not quite there.

He was performing well by every measure the program had. What the program didn't have a measure for was this.

The grade doesn't capture the weight. And the program isn't looking for it.

How Isolation Gets Built In

Isolation within teacher education is not simply a function of numbers.

It is produced through patterns embedded in curriculum, faculty composition, and institutional norms. When course content consistently centers dominant perspectives as foundational, when race is engaged only intermittently, when leadership spaces lack diversity—a message is communicated clearly: some identities are central here. Others are accommodated.

These signals accumulate. In syllabi that omit critical perspectives. In classroom discussions that engage race without fully interrogating it. In faculty interactions that are well-intentioned but limited in their ability to engage Black men's lived realities.

No single moment defines the environment. The pattern does.

Over time, sustained interpretation becomes fatigue. Belonging doesn't erode through a single moment. It diminishes through repetition—through the steady accumulation of interactions that require adjustment, translation, and restraint.

This is what makes isolation in teacher education so insidious. It doesn't look like isolation. It looks like functioning. The candidate is present, engaged, performing. What isn't visible is what that performance requires.

REAL TALK

When Black men build community in teacher education—the group chats, the informal study sessions, the check-ins after hard classes—that is not supplemental social activity. That is infrastructure. That is belonging being constructed in the absence of institutional design. It is impressive. It is also evidence of institutional failure.

What Belonging Actually Requires

Belonging is a condition that directly shapes participation, intellectual risk-taking, and long-term retention.

When institutions fail to design for belonging, they inadvertently design for attrition.

This book proposes a framework for fixing that—the C.A.R.E. Model, introduced in Chapter 12. Community. Access. Representation. Equity. These are not aspirations. They are design specifications. Each one addresses a gap that shows up in every chapter of this book.

Belonging is not a bonus. It is a condition. And conditions can be engineered.

Designing for belonging requires intentional structures: cohort models that connect Black male candidates across a program's timeline, mentorship systems that are structured rather than incidental, curriculum that positions diverse intellectual traditions as foundational, and faculty diversification that includes actual authority—not just presence.

When belonging is designed rather than incidental, candidates engage more fully. They take intellectual risks. They pursue leadership opportunities. They envision futures beyond the classroom.

The question is not whether Black men can create belonging in the absence of structure. They already do. The question is whether institutions are willing to take responsibility for designing it.

What happens when belonging is designed rather than incidental is not a hypothetical. Programs that have made these investments—structured cohorts, intentional mentorship, diverse faculty with genuine authority—report measurably different outcomes. Candidates persist at higher rates. They pursue leadership more frequently. They report stronger professional identity.

These outcomes are not mysterious. They are the predictable product of environments designed to produce them.

The inverse is equally predictable. Environments not designed for belonging produce the attrition and isolation that have characterized Black male participation in teacher education for decades. Not as an accident. As a consequence of design decisions that were never examined.

REAL TALK

If your program doesn't know your name by your second semester, that is not a minor oversight. That is a belonging problem. You are allowed to name it as such—to an advisor, in a survey, in an exit interview. Programs that don't hear it can't fix it. And programs that do hear it and don't act on it have told you something important about their actual priorities.

PLAYBOOK MOVE

- Build your network deliberately. Identify two to four people who share your context and invest in those relationships with consistency and reciprocity.
- When isolation feels personal, name the structural conditions producing it. Write them down. That reframe protects your confidence.
- Use every available institutional resource—multicultural centers, student organizations, affinity networks. These are strategic infrastructure, not social extras.
- Track what your informal network provides that the institution does not. That gap is data—and a conversation worth having with someone in a position to respond.
- If your program has a student governance structure or advisory committee, consider participating. The most direct way to influence institutional design is to be inside the conversations where design decisions are made.

CHAPTER 6

Institutional Bias and Structural Gatekeeping

Bias in teacher education rarely shows up as a confrontation.

It shows up as a pattern.

It lives in feedback language, evaluation criteria, which perspectives get centered in curriculum, and which get treated as supplemental. It operates quietly—through what is normalized, what goes unchallenged, and whose interpretation of events gets treated as the default.

> ***Standards within teacher education are often presented as neutral, yet they are rooted in cultural norms defined without Black men at the center.***

HOW BIAS OPERATES IN EVALUATION

Evaluation in teacher education is not a purely objective process. It is interpretive.

The rubric exists, but so does the evaluator. And the evaluator brings assumptions about what competence looks like, what authority sounds like, and what professionalism means.

Black men frequently find that their participation gets interpreted differently than their peers'. Critical inquiry becomes confrontation. Direct communication becomes aggressive tone. Assertiveness gets coded as resistance. These interpretations show up in written feedback, observational assessments, and informal conversations that carry professional consequence.

Individually, each feels like a style note. Collectively, they shape trajectory.

When interpretation is uneven, opportunity becomes uneven. Recommendations get shaped by perception. Placement decisions reflect assumptions. Perceptions of readiness get influenced by factors that have nothing to do with instructional skill.

Bias, in this form, doesn't announce itself. It accumulates in the record. And over time, that record follows people.

By the time you see the pattern clearly, it has already shaped the path.

SCENARIO: THE FEEDBACK THAT DOESN'T ADD UP

Two candidates teach similar lessons in the same week. Both receive positive evaluations. One is told her directness shows confidence and leadership. The other is told his directness comes across as "too intense" and that he should work on "softening his approach." The lessons were comparable. The feedback was not. He sits with this. He doesn't know whether to push back, adjust, or absorb it and move on. He chooses to absorb it—for now. But the pattern stays with him.

The Field Placement Problem

Field placements are where perception carries the most weight.

Placement decisions, continuation decisions, and evaluations often hinge on interpretations of "fit." That word does a lot of work. Fit for whom? Defined by whom?

When a cooperating teacher is uncomfortable with a Black male candidate's presence and that discomfort gets translated into professional concern, the criteria for belonging become unstable.

Perception overrides performance. For Black men already navigating heightened scrutiny, these moments reinforce the conditional nature of their position.

Economic structures compound this. Unpaid field placements, certification exam fees, application costs, reduced work hours—many Black men navigate these demands while maintaining employment and supporting family responsibilities. Financial strain is not peripheral. It shapes access to time, resources, and opportunities. When programs assume economic flexibility as a baseline, they privilege candidates with material security.

REAL TALK

"Fit" is one of the most dangerous words in teacher education. It sounds professional. It functions as cover. When your performance is strong but your fit is questioned, ask specifically: What behaviors are you observing? What outcomes are not being met? Push for concrete answers. Vague concerns about fit—without specific evidence—deserve specific questions in return.

LICENSURE AS A STRUCTURAL FILTER

Standardized licensure assessments are positioned as objective measures of readiness. They are not neutral.

They are designed. And design reflects priorities. These exams consistently prioritize dominant cultural norms and specific forms of academic literacy. They rarely assess relational capacity, cultural responsiveness, or the ability to build trust across diverse contexts.

The cumulative impact of these dynamics is significant. Black men engage in ongoing interpretive labor—assessing whether feedback reflects performance or perception, whether opportunities are based on merit or influenced by bias, whether advancement is truly accessible. This continuous interpretation requires energy that could otherwise go toward learning, innovation, and leadership development.

The issue is not access alone. It is trajectory—who is stabilized, who is sponsored, and who is ultimately recognized as an architect of the field.

What institutions often fail to acknowledge is that the interpretive labor required to navigate structural bias doesn't leave candidates when they enter classrooms. It shapes how Black men approach the profession itself.

How much they trust institutional feedback. How freely they pursue opportunities that require advocacy. How readily they envision themselves in leadership roles. The downstream effects of consistent misrecognition are not limited to individual moments of frustration. They compound across time.

The question is not how Black men can better navigate these systems. The question is how these systems are designed—and how that design distributes access, authority, and opportunity. Not only who enters. But how those programs sustain, support, and position those who enter.

REAL TALK

The licensure exam is a gatekeeping structure, not an objective measure of teaching ability. Study it like you're learning a language—because you are. The language is not neutral. And knowing it doesn't mean you agree with it. It means you've decided to pass through the gate on your own terms.

PLAYBOOK MOVE

- When feedback feels unclear or inconsistent, request specificity in writing. "Can you point to the specific behaviors in my lesson that concern you?" Vague feedback is harder to address—and harder to dispute.

- Before field placements begin, ask explicitly: What does success look like? Who evaluates it? What is the process if concerns arise? Clarity before problems emerge is protection.

- For licensure exams, study the format as much as the content. These tests have a specific logic. Learn it.

- Track financial barriers and report them. Many programs have emergency funds and fee waivers that are not proactively offered. Ask directly.

- Request a mid-semester check-in with your supervisor if feedback has been sparse or unclear. Don't wait for the end-of-term evaluation to discover that perception has been forming without your input.

CHAPTER 7

The Disciplinarian Myth and the Narrowing of Professional Identity

Before many Black men have fully defined who they are as educators, others have already begun to define it for them.

The definition rarely arrives as an insult. It arrives as a compliment.

"The students really respond to you." "You have a natural authority in the room." "You're exactly what that challenging class needs."

These things may be true. The problem is what gets said next. And what never gets said at all.

> ***Affirmation becomes assignment. And assignment, over time, becomes limitation.***

WHAT THE DISCIPLINARIAN MYTH IS

The Disciplinarian Myth is the persistent belief that Black men's primary professional value in schools is their ability to manage behavior, establish order, and stabilize classroom environments.

It assumes authority is inherent. That presence alone commands respect. That behavioral management is the most significant contribution they offer.

The issue is not the capacity. Many Black men demonstrate genuine strength in classroom management. The issue is the reduction. When this becomes the dominant lens through which their work is understood, a multidimensional professional identity narrows to a single function.

Control is elevated. Cognition, design, and intellectual contribution receive less attention.

This narrowing often appears as praise.

That is the difficulty. The praise is genuine. The recognition is real. The man in front of the classroom is doing something valuable. But the framing of that value—when it consistently centers control and excludes cognition—shapes what opportunities follow.

It shapes what gets funded. Who gets recommended for curriculum leadership. Who gets invited into research conversations. Who gets encouraged to pursue doctoral study. The affirmation is narrow. And narrow affirmation, repeated over time, becomes a ceiling.

Praised into a corner. That is the pattern.

A candidate gets asked to support the challenging classroom because of his perceived authority. Feedback highlights composure and command, while offering little engagement with instructional design. Opportunities align with behavior management rather than broader dimensions of teaching. What is framed as affirmation gradually shapes expectation.

SCENARIO: THE PLACEMENT ASSIGNMENT

Three candidates are assigned to student teaching placements. Two go to stable mid-level classes. The third—the only Black man in the cohort—is placed in a class the department describes as "high need" and "a strong match for his energy and presence." His skills in instructional design, which his coursework grades reflect clearly, are not mentioned in the placement rationale. His evaluation praises his classroom management. His lesson planning receives two sentences. He wonders if anyone in this program has actually read his unit plans.

HOW PRAISE OPERATES AS A BOUNDARY

Nobody tells a Black male candidate his thinking doesn't matter. They just keep asking him to handle the hard class, the disruptive student, the difficult moment.

Over time, responsibilities cluster. Pathways into curriculum, research, and policy become less visible—not through formal exclusion, but through patterned omission. Praise keeps Black men close to students but distant from institutional influence. The role is recognized. Its scope stays narrow.

Institutions can correct this. Give feedback that matches the full scope of practice. Engage lesson planning with the same depth as classroom management. Invite Black male candidates into curriculum conversations and research opportunities. Ask what they want to build—not only where they can be deployed.

This is not a question of capability. It is a question of recognition—and of what that recognition makes possible.

REAL TALK

If every opportunity coming your way involves managing behavior or stabilizing a difficult space, examine that pattern. It may reflect your real strength. It may also reflect what the institution has decided your strength is. Those are not always the same thing. Know the difference.

EXPANDING THE FRAME

Discipline and design are not in opposition.

Relational strength does not diminish intellectual rigor. Classroom presence and scholarly contribution can coexist. Black men navigating these environments are aware of these constraints. Some move within them strategically. Others challenge them directly—pursuing research, engaging in curriculum work, seeking mentorship that affirms their full range.

Both responses are legitimate. Both require that you first see the frame clearly.

The Disciplinarian Myth is not corrected by assigning Black men to different classrooms. It is corrected by examining the evaluative frameworks that produce it and redesigning them to reflect the full scope of what effective teaching requires.

This means naming instructional design, theoretical grounding, and curricular thinking as evaluation priorities in every observation cycle—not only when the evaluator finds them noteworthy. It means building professional development structures that position all candidates as intellectuals, not only those whose authority is not already assumed.

The question is not whether they can manage a classroom. The question is whether teacher education is prepared to recognize them as architects of the profession itself.

REAL TALK

You can be the best classroom manager in your cohort and still be the most underestimated scholar. Those are not contradictions. They are the product of a system that assigns value unevenly. Build the portfolio that documents who you actually are—not just how you function in the spaces they put you in.

PLAYBOOK MOVE

- When feedback consistently centers presence and behavior management, ask directly: "What feedback do you have on my instructional design?" Name what you want evaluated.
- Build a professional portfolio that foregrounds your intellectual work—unit plans, lesson rationales, written reflections on pedagogy. Make your thinking visible and hard to overlook.
- If you are consistently placed in high-need classrooms while peers with comparable skills are not, name the pattern. Ask how placement decisions are made.
- Seek mentors who engage your ideas, not just your presence. The mentor who asks about your research interests is the one to invest in.
- Consider how you might eventually contribute to curriculum conversations or research initiatives within your program. Leadership begins before formal roles.

CHAPTER 8

Counter-Spaces and the Construction of Community

When institutional design fails to center Black men, they build what is missing.

Community rarely begins as a formal initiative. It begins quietly—often in moments that appear small but carry meaning.

A glance across a classroom after a difficult discussion. A brief exchange outside a seminar. A moment where two people recognize—without saying it explicitly—that something just happened and neither is sure how to process it alone.

> *What begins as connection does not remain incidental. It develops. It takes shape. Over time, it becomes infrastructure.*

How Community Starts

"Was that just me? Did you notice that?"

Those two questions are the beginning of counter-community. Through these exchanges, experience shifts. What felt personal becomes recognizable as shared. What felt like a misread in one moment gets confirmed as a pattern across several. The weight changes when it is no longer carried alone.

As connections deepen, they take on structure. What starts as informal conversation evolves into intentional support. Peers become accountability partners. Time outside class becomes space for preparation and strategy. The men in these networks review lesson plans together, prepare for certification exams collectively, rehearse responses to anticipated feedback.

What institutions leave ambiguous, the community works to make legible.

That legibility matters more than institutions acknowledge. Knowing how to decode an evaluation rubric, how to approach a difficult supervisor, how to navigate a certification requirement—this knowledge is power. When it circulates within a community rather than through official advising channels, it reveals a structural gap.

Institutions have this knowledge. They simply haven't organized it in ways that reach every candidate equitably.

REAL TALK

Every piece of navigation knowledge you had to figure out on your own—about a supervisor, an evaluation rubric, a certification deadline, a faculty relationship—is a piece of knowledge the advising system was supposed to give you. It didn't. So you found it another way. That is resourcefulness. It is also evidence of a gap. Name both.

SCENARIO: THE GROUP CHAT THAT BECAME A SUPPORT SYSTEM

It started as a way to coordinate carpooling to a mandatory Saturday session. Within two weeks, the chat had become something else entirely. Lesson plans were shared and critiqued. Feedback from supervisors was deconstructed collectively. Graduate school opportunities were posted. Certification exam study guides were exchanged. When one member got a confusing evaluation, the group spent two hours that evening helping him figure out what the evaluator actually meant—and what to do about it. No faculty member organized this. No program initiative created it. Five Black men in a cohort built it because they needed it.

WHAT THESE SPACES ACTUALLY DO

Counter-spaces do several things simultaneously that formal institutions often don't.

They provide interpretation. Feedback that arrives coded or ambiguous gets processed collectively. Institutional language that obscures more than it clarifies gets translated. What could have been absorbed as self-doubt gets reframed.

They expand professional imagination. In environments where intellectual capacity is affirmed rather than questioned, ambition widens. Conversations begin to include graduate study, research pathways, leadership roles. These possibilities are often surfaced through dialogue within the community—not through formal program structures.

Leadership, in this context, is not assigned. It is constructed.

REAL TALK

The community you build in this program may outlast the program itself. Those connections often become the most durable professional network of your career—people who share your context, understand your trajectory, and will advocate for you in rooms you haven't entered yet. Treat those relationships with the same strategic intentionality you bring to your coursework.

THE LIMITATION—AND WHAT IT REVEALS

These counter-spaces are powerful. They are also compensatory.

They exist because formal structures do not consistently provide what is needed. When belonging depends on informal networks, institutions are not required to change. Students adapt while systems remain intact.

The most enduring counter-spaces become intentionally intergenerational. Men further along begin mentoring those who are entering. What began as necessity becomes sustainability.

Every semester that passes without formal community infrastructure is a semester in which individual Black male candidates expend energy building what should already exist. That energy has a cost. And it is a cost the institution is effectively transferring to its most vulnerable candidates.

If Black men can build this level of relational infrastructure without formal support, what becomes possible when institutions design for it intentionally?

The community is both a solution and a diagnosis. What it provides points directly to what the institution has yet to build.

PLAYBOOK MOVE

- Form your core network early and deliberately. Identify two to four people who share your context. Invest in those relationships with consistency.
- Use the group strategically. Bring lesson plans. Bring confusing feedback. Bring opportunities you've found. Treat the group as a professional development structure.
- When you're further along, reach back. Share what you've learned. Don't hoard navigation knowledge.
- Document what your informal network provides that the institution does not. That gap is evidence for a formal mentorship program or redesigned advising model.

CHAPTER 9

Mentorship and the Stabilization of Trajectory

Informal community provides solidarity. Mentorship provides direction.

These are not the same thing. And both are necessary.

Across Black men's experiences in teacher education, one pattern surfaces with unusual clarity: progress accelerates when mentorship is present. Not a program-assigned advisor who meets quarterly. A mentor who sees the full picture, understands the institutional terrain, and is invested in where you are going.

> ***A mentor sees beyond stereotype, beyond misinterpretation, and beyond the constrained roles that are often implicitly assigned.***

WHAT MENTORSHIP ACTUALLY DOES

Most people understand mentorship as encouragement. For Black men navigating teacher education, it functions at a deeper structural level.

It is trajectory-shaping. It influences how individuals interpret their experiences, how they position themselves within the profession, and how they move through pathways that are often unclear or unevenly structured.

Mentors are often the first people to recognize intellectual capacity before the institution does. That recognition—early, specific, grounded in a real understanding of your work—changes what you believe is possible.

A mentor sees you clearly when the system does not.

SCENARIO: THE CONVERSATION THAT CHANGED DIRECTION

Andre was three semesters into his program and performing solidly—but operating within a narrow sense of what his future could look like. He imagined himself in a middle school classroom in his home district. His advisor had never suggested anything beyond that. One afternoon, a faculty member who had read his written reflections asked him to stay after class. She told him his theoretical analysis was graduate-level thinking. She asked if he had ever considered doctoral study. He hadn't. Not because he lacked the interest—but because no one had ever made it feel possible. That conversation reoriented his entire professional imagination.

The Translation Function

One of the most critical functions of mentorship is translation.

Teacher education operates through implicit norms that are rarely made explicit. When feedback feels misaligned—when you know your intent and the evaluation doesn't reflect it—a mentor helps decode that gap. They clarify what the institution is actually looking for beneath the coded language. They distinguish between critique about your practice and critique about how your practice is being perceived.

They help you respond to both without requiring self-erasure.

The intervention is not corrective. It is interpretive.

Mentors also name possibilities that formal program structures often don't. Graduate study. Research pathways. Curriculum leadership. Policy engagement. Faculty roles. These possibilities are frequently opened through mentorship—not through advising appointments.

REAL TALK

The mentor who tells you what the institution really means when it gives you confusing feedback is one of the most valuable relationships you can build. Not because the institution's framing is always right—sometimes it isn't—but because understanding the framing is the first step to deciding how to respond to it. You cannot navigate a system you cannot read.

WHEN MENTORSHIP IS ABSENT

The absence of mentorship reveals its structural importance.

Those without it describe greater uncertainty in interpreting feedback and fewer invitations into professional networks and opportunities. Without mentorship, pathways into graduate study, research, and leadership are harder to access—not because they don't exist, but because no one has pointed toward them.

Mentors also redistribute access to institutional knowledge that is otherwise distributed unevenly. They know which evaluation criteria are fixed and which have flexibility. They know what graduate programs actually look for. They know how professional networks function in practice. This is not secret information. It is unevenly accessible information. Mentors change that.

Mentorship does not simply prepare Black men to enter classrooms. At its best, it positions them to influence the systems that prepare educators.

PLAYBOOK MOVE

- Don't wait for mentorship to find you. Identify one or two faculty members whose work aligns with yours and pursue those relationships with intentionality. Come with specific questions.
- Make your thinking visible to potential mentors. Share written work. Engage their scholarship in class. Mentors invest in people whose intellectual engagement they can see.
- If mentorship within your program is limited, look beyond it. Professional organizations, academic conferences, and alumni networks are all legitimate sources.
- When you receive mentorship, receive it actively. Come prepared. Follow through on guidance. Report back on outcomes.
- As you gain experience, consider systematizing your navigational insights into resources for others. What took you a semester to figure out should take the next person a week.

CHAPTER 10

Strategic Navigation Within Institutional Systems

By the midpoint of their programs, many Black men arrive at a realization that is rarely stated directly but consistently understood.

Institutions operate through two simultaneous systems: the visible and the invisible.

The visible system is documented—syllabi, rubrics, certification benchmarks, evaluation criteria. The invisible system runs beneath it—norms about tone, timing, perception, and how interpretation shapes outcome.

Mastery of both is what trajectory actually requires. And mastery of the second is never taught.

> ***What appears structured and transparent on the surface reveals a more complex reality in practice. Success is shaped by tone, timing, perception, and interpretation.***

When Participation Becomes Strategy

Black men in teacher education develop what might be called institutional fluency.

The ability to read how the system actually operates versus how it presents itself. They recognize patterns in how feedback is delivered, how critique is received, how authority moves through educational spaces. They learn when to speak and how to frame what they say based on a real-time assessment of how it will land.

Follow-up questions begin serving a different purpose—not just seeking clarification, but positioning. Communication becomes more deliberate in writing, where clarity protects intent. When feedback is unclear, it gets documented. When expectations feel ambiguous, they get clarified in advance.

What appears as over-preparation is, in practice, strategy.

SCENARIO: THE EMAIL THAT TOOK FORTY-FIVE MINUTES TO WRITE

After a tense seminar discussion, Jerome drafted a follow-up email to his professor. Not because anything had gone wrong on paper—he had said what he meant—but because he had noticed the room shift after his comment, and he knew that perception would follow him into his next evaluation. The email was three paragraphs. It clarified his argument, connected it to the reading, and asked a substantive follow-up question. It took forty-five minutes to write because every sentence was measured. His roommate sent a three-sentence email the same evening and was done in five minutes. Both approaches were legitimate. Only one of them was a necessity.

Reading the Room—Consistently

Discernment becomes essential.

Not every moment requires response. Not every comment requires correction. The men in these environments learn to read the difference. In some moments, speaking advances the conversation. In others, it carries consequence without impact.

Agency, in this context, is not simply expression. It is timing.

In classroom discussions, strategy takes the form of precision. Lived experience is not removed from the analysis—but it is framed.

Connected to theory, to scholarship, to frameworks that require engagement on intellectual terms. The goal is not to soften perspective. It is to make it harder to dismiss.

> **REAL TALK**
>
> Strategic navigation is not assimilation. You are not abandoning your identity or your convictions. You are making informed decisions about how to deploy them within a system you understand. There is a meaningful difference between choosing how to enter a room and letting the room choose who you are. One is strategy. The other is compromise. Know which one you're doing.

Navigation Becomes Collective

What is learned through individual navigation does not stay individual.

Black men share what they learn—about specific supervisors, evaluation language, how to prepare for particular requirements. Templates get exchanged. Strategies get discussed. What was once unevenly distributed becomes accessible within the community. Navigation becomes collective rather than isolated.

Still, this level of awareness carries a cost. Monitoring tone, reading rooms, calibrating responses, anticipating how something will be received before it is spoken—this is constant work. It does not appear on a transcript. It is not factored into anyone's assessment of workload. Yet it remains essential to navigating these environments successfully.

Strategic navigation transforms reactive endurance into informed positioning.

The candidates producing this navigation knowledge are doing institutional work. They are filling a gap that formal advising structures were supposed to fill.

That labor deserves to be absorbed into institutional design rather than left to be rediscovered by each new cohort. The knowledge exists. The candidates are generating it.

The institutional fluency Black men develop through sustained navigation is not a consolation prize. It is legitimate professional knowledge with direct value in every educational leadership context.

PLAYBOOK MOVE

- After any high-stakes interaction, debrief it in writing within 24 hours. What happened? What did you notice? What was said and what was implied? This documentation sharpens pattern recognition.
- For important written communication, develop a drafting practice. Write freely first, then revise for strategic clarity. Ask: Is my argument grounded? Is my intent visible? Could this be misread?
- Identify which evaluators and supervisors see your work most clearly and invest in those relationships.
- Share navigation strategies within your network. What you've learned has value to someone coming behind you. Distribute it.
- The strategic work of navigating teacher education is real intellectual work. Name it as such.

CHAPTER 11

The Emotional Cost of Sustained Navigation

By the later stages of teacher education, many Black men appear composed.

They participate with precision, perform well in field placements, pass certification exams, meet institutional benchmarks.

From the outside, the story reads as progress.

What remains largely unseen is the cost required to sustain that composure.

> ***Success does not remove strain. It often conceals it.***

THE MOMENT THAT STAYS WITH YOU

After a post-observation conference that had gone well by every formal measure, one candidate received positive feedback on his classroom presence and pacing.

Then came the final note: he should soften his delivery slightly, to avoid being perceived as intimidating.

He acknowledged the feedback. It was not unfamiliar. Walking back to his car, he replayed the lesson. He had followed the rubric. His tone had been steady. No student had expressed discomfort. Still, he reconsidered how he had spoken, how he had moved, how he might be read differently.

By the time he reached home, the fatigue had set in. Not from the lesson itself. From the interpretation of it.

That is the kind of exhaustion that doesn't show up on any rubric.

SCENARIO: THE END OF A HARD SEMESTER

By December, Kevin had completed every requirement and was on track to graduate in the spring. He had also spent sixteen weeks monitoring his tone in every seminar discussion, tracking the room before he spoke in class, recalibrating after feedback that felt more about perception than performance, and being the person other people looked to when conversations about race became uncomfortable. Nobody had asked him to do most of this. The program had simply produced conditions where not doing it felt riskier than doing it. He was fine on paper. Underneath that, he was exhausted in a way that a semester break alone wouldn't fix.

Naming the Exhaustion

The fatigue Black men describe rarely ties to a single incident.

It accumulates. Produced through sustained vigilance. Reading rooms before speaking. Calculating how much of oneself can be visible in any given interaction. Adjusting expression to remain legible within the space.

W.E.B. Du Bois named this dynamic more than a century ago. Double consciousness. The experience of seeing yourself while simultaneously tracking how you are seen through a racialized lens. In teacher education, that awareness becomes professionalized.

You are not only learning pedagogy. You are learning how your pedagogy will be interpreted. The cognitive work doubles. And it does not turn off.

Scholars describe this as racial battle fatigue. The accumulated psychological and physiological toll of ongoing racialized stress. It is not fragility. It is the predictable result of sustained effort within environments that require more interpretive work from some than from others.

REAL TALK

The exhaustion is real, and it is not a sign that you are not built for this. It is a sign that you have been doing more work than the rubric accounts for. Naming that—to yourself, to your support network, and when appropriate, to the institution—is not weakness. It is accuracy. You cannot address what you haven't named correctly.

Persistence Is Not the Same as Fine

The men who move through these programs and complete them are not doing so because the strain was minimal.

They are doing so despite it. Endurance and ease are not the same thing.

There is also tension between recognition and support. Black men are frequently affirmed for leadership, presence, and commitment. Yet that recognition does not consistently translate into sponsorship, protection, or expanded opportunity. Being seen without being structurally supported creates dissonance. Recognition without redistribution of access or power remains incomplete.

When belonging requires constant awareness, the system extracts more than it gives.

The goal is not to stop persisting. It is to name the conditions that make persistence necessary—and to work toward systems where endurance is not the prerequisite for success.

Many Black men in teacher education see clearly what could be different. How mentorship could be structured. How evaluation could be recalibrated. How curriculum could expand. To hold that vision while continuing to move within the current system requires disciplined restraint.

That vision does not make the fatigue disappear. But it gives it direction. And direction, over time, becomes change.

PLAYBOOK MOVE

- Name your experience accurately. If the semester was hard not because of the academic demands but because of sustained interpretive labor—say that, at least to yourself. Accurate naming is the first step to accurate response.
- Build in deliberate recovery. What restores your clarity? Schedule it with the same commitment you give your coursework.
- Identify one or two people who understand what you're navigating and who you can debrief with honestly. Not every burden needs to be managed alone.
- Know when to escalate. If you are experiencing documented patterns of inequitable evaluation or hostile climate, most institutions have formal processes. Know what they are.
- Understand the difference between coping and recovery. Coping keeps you functional. Recovery restores your capacity. Both matter. Only one of them is sustainable long-term.

CHAPTER 12

From Adaptation to Architecture: The C.A.R.E. Model

Teacher education does not lack intention. It lacks alignment.

Across institutions, there are stated commitments to diversity, inclusion, and equity. Recruitment expands. Initiatives launch. Statements get published. And still, Black men continue to navigate programs that require continuous adjustment, offer inconsistent support, and produce uneven outcomes.

The problem is not whether institutions care. The problem is whether they are built to sustain what they claim to value.

Equity approached as a series of interventions rather than a matter of system design will always produce short-term gains and long-term stagnation.

> *The shift this chapter makes is fundamental: the question is no longer how individuals can better navigate teacher education. The question is how teacher education must be redesigned so that navigation is no longer the prerequisite for belonging.*

INTRODUCING THE C.A.R.E. MODEL

Here's what became clear through this research: the problems Black men face in teacher education are not random. They cluster around the same four gaps, in the same four areas, across institution after institution.

Community is absent or informal. Access breaks down mid-program. Representation stops at the door. Equity gets stated but not measured.

The C.A.R.E. Model names those four gaps and provides a structure for closing them.

C.A.R.E.—Community, Access, Representation, Equity—provides institutions with a way to move from intention to implementation. These four dimensions are not independent. When one is misaligned, the others are affected. Institutions cannot prioritize one while neglecting the rest and expect sustained outcomes.

Community	Belonging must be engineered, not incidental. Structured cohorts, formalized mentorship, and embedded support networks move community from informal compensation to institutional infrastructure.
Access	Access is not only about entry. It extends through completion and into employment. Financial support, advising alignment, certification preparation, and workforce transition must function as a continuous pathway.
Representation	Presence alone does not redistribute power. Representation must extend into faculty roles, curriculum design, governance, and decision-making. It is achieved when Black men can shape the direction of the field.
Equity	Equity without accountability is aspiration. Institutions must examine how policies and practices are experienced, not just intended. Disparities must trigger redesign, not explanation.

Community as Infrastructure

Think about what you actually used to get through this program.

Not the advising appointments. Not the orientation sessions. The group chat. The study session that turned into a two-hour debrief. The friend who explained what the evaluator actually meant when the feedback made no sense.

That was community. And you built it yourself. Because the program didn't.

In most programs, Black men build community in response to its absence. That community is powerful. It is also compensatory. The C.A.R.E. Model reframes community as something institutions design deliberately—structured cohorts, formalized mentorship, belonging treated as a condition that must be built and maintained, not a byproduct of participation.

Access: Who Makes It Through

How many people do you know who left a program not because they weren't capable, but because the timing didn't work? Because the placement was unpaid and rent was due?

That is an access problem. And it has nothing to do with ability.

Access measured only at the point of admission is incomplete. Financial strain, certification barriers, and rigid program structures determine whether candidates can continue—not just whether they are capable. Scholarships, stipends, exam support, and flexible sequencing are not supplemental. They are the architecture of equitable access.

SCENARIO: THE SEMESTER HE ALMOST LEFT

David was two semesters from finishing when his car broke down. The unpaid student teaching placement was forty minutes away. No car meant no placement. No placement meant no certification. He called his advisor. The advisor expressed sympathy and suggested the emergency fund. The fund had a six-week processing time. The placement started in ten days. He found a solution—borrowed money, a friend with a flexible schedule. But it took three days he didn't have and energy he couldn't spare. He finished. But he almost didn't. Not because he couldn't teach. Because the program wasn't designed to hold him.

Representation: Past the Front Door

Here's the test: Can a Black man in your program look around and see someone who looks like him teaching the course, designing the curriculum, sitting in the room where decisions get made?

If the answer is no—or rarely—that is not a diversity problem. That is a representation problem. And they are not the same thing.

Representation requires the authority to shape outcomes—to influence how knowledge is defined, how professionalism is interpreted, and how future educators are prepared. Presence in enrollment statistics without presence in faculty governance is not representation. It is optics.

Equity: Show Me the Data

Most programs will tell you they are committed to equity. Ask them to show you the data. Watch what happens.

Some will pull up a report. Others will get quiet. The ones who get quiet are the ones whose commitment lives in the language of the mission statement and nowhere else.

Equity requires institutions to ask and answer difficult questions about persistence rates, progression patterns, and evaluation outcomes, disaggregated by race and gender. When disparities are identified, they must lead to redesign. Not explanation.

Alignment is no longer optional. It is the condition for whether teacher education can fulfill its stated purpose.

When institutions implement the C.A.R.E. Model with intention, the results follow a clear pattern. Recruitment improves because pathways are clear. Persistence improves because support is consistent. Representation deepens because authority is distributed more equitably. Outcomes strengthen because systems are accountable to data rather than rhetoric.

That is the logic of alignment. Each dimension strengthens the others. When one is missing, the others are weakened.

Teacher education has more capacity for transformation than it has chosen to use. The C.A.R.E. Model doesn't introduce a new idea. It introduces a new expectation: that institutions align their practices with their stated commitments—and measure themselves against outcomes, not intentions.

SCENARIO: WHAT ALIGNMENT ACTUALLY LOOKS LIKE

A program at a regional university redesigned its advising structure after tracking that Black male candidates were leaving at twice the rate of their peers. They added a peer cohort model, created a paid clinical placement option, hired two Black faculty in the first year, and began disaggregating persistence data by race. Within two years, the gap had closed. Not through a diversity statement. By treating four specific gaps as design problems with design solutions.

PLAYBOOK MOVE

- Use the C.A.R.E. framework to evaluate your own program. Where is community structured? Where does access break down? Where is representation present without authority? Where is equity stated but not practiced?

- When advocating for change, use the language of design. "The advising structure doesn't consistently support candidates who are working while enrolled" is more actionable than "I feel unsupported."

- If you are in a position to contribute to program improvement—through a student representative role, survey, or exit interview—be specific about which dimension needs the most attention, and why.

- Share the C.A.R.E. framework with colleagues. A shared analytical language for institutional dynamics is itself a form of community infrastructure.

CHAPTER 13

Becoming Visible: Rewriting the Future of Teacher Education

Visibility, as this book uses the term, is not about being seen.

It is about being understood as a contributor. Having lived experience engaged as meaningful. Having intellectual authority recognized as legitimate. Having presence translate into influence over how the field defines itself.

That is the kind of visibility that changes institutions. And it does not happen passively.

> ***Becoming visible is not about occupying space. It is about shaping it.***

WHAT THE PATTERNS REVEAL

Black men move through teacher education spaces where their presence is acknowledged before their insight is fully engaged.

They are interpreted quickly and understood more gradually. When they describe hypervisibility, constraint, or the need for strategic navigation, they are not speaking only about personal experience. They are offering a lens through which institutions can examine how expectations are communicated, how evaluation is experienced, and where the gap between intention and lived reality must be closed.

Their experiences are not anecdotal. They are diagnostic.

EXPANDING WHAT COUNTS AS KNOWLEDGE

For too long, teacher preparation has privileged detachment and neutrality as markers of rigor.

Lived experience has been treated as secondary—less generalizable, less theoretical, less legitimate. A more expansive approach recognizes lived experience as expertise that deepens understanding of teaching, learning, and institutional context.

When this perspective is integrated across coursework rather than isolated into occasional diversity discussions, it strengthens how future educators are prepared to lead in complex environments.

Evaluation practices must evolve alongside this expanded understanding. Professionalism, as currently interpreted, requires examination. Feedback must become more transparent, more specific, and more clearly connected to observable practice. Field experiences must be designed with intentionality, ensuring all candidates have access to opportunities that develop both instructional skill and leadership capacity.

SCENARIO: THE DISCUSSION THAT COULD HAVE GONE FURTHER

A Black male preservice teacher offers an observation grounded in both theory and his own experience teaching in an under-resourced school. The professor acknowledges the comment warmly and moves on. A different professor—one who saw it as a theoretical contribution—would have paused: "That's a significant pedagogical argument. Can you say more about how that connects to the framework we read this week?" That pause changes what the class discussion produces. It also changes what the candidate believes about where his thinking belongs in the conversation.

That second version of the professor is not a unicorn. They exist. The question is whether the institution builds conditions that produce more of them.

What you bring into the classroom—your analysis, your framework, your reading of the room—is not anecdotal. It is theoretical. And claiming it, out loud, in the room, is part of becoming visible.

VISIBILITY AS POSITIONING

Becoming visible moves lived experience from the margins of institutional conversation to a central role in shaping how the profession understands itself.

The future of teacher education will be shaped by how institutions respond—not through rhetoric, but through decisions. How policies are revised. How programs are structured. How accountability is enacted.

When evaluation becomes clearer, when curriculum reflects a wider range of intellectual traditions, and when belonging is intentionally designed, the profession becomes stronger. Not in spite of Black men's full participation. Because of it.

Visibility that produces institutional change requires positioning at multiple levels simultaneously. Through individual relationships—mentors who name possibilities, faculty who engage scholarship on its analytical merits. Through program structures—evaluation criteria that reward the full range of teaching capacity, curriculum that treats Black intellectual traditions as foundational. Through governance—Black educators in positions where they define standards, allocate resources, and shape what the field considers legitimate knowledge.

Each of these levels requires intentional action. None of them happens through representation alone.

Hiring a Black faculty member does not automatically produce structural visibility if that faculty member remains peripheral to curriculum design. Recruiting Black male candidates does not produce transformation if the program that receives them is unchanged. Becoming visible, in the fullest sense this book intends, is the work of changing the conditions that determine who gets recognized and what that recognition makes possible.

PLAYBOOK MOVE

- Assert your intellectual authority in every appropriate context. When your insight is theoretical, name the framework. When grounded in experience, connect it explicitly to the scholarship.
- Seek programs, professors, and environments that engage your thinking on its own terms. Not every space will. Find the ones that do.
- Visibility that ends at the classroom door has limited systemic impact. Think about how your presence in one space creates access to conversations that might produce change in another.
- When you complete your program, consider how you will continue to contribute to the field—through research, writing, professional advocacy, or mentoring those who come after you.

CHAPTER 14

Healing, Hope, and Reclaiming the Profession

At some point in the journey, persistence alone is no longer sufficient.

After navigating misinterpretation, strategic restraint, and the steady discipline required to move through spaces that do not always fully reflect your experience, something begins to shift.

Not all at once. Through reflection. Through conversation. Through moments of clarity that reframe what you have been carrying.

That clarity reveals something essential: the tension so often internalized was never evidence of inadequacy. It was a reflection of misalignment between individual experience and institutional context.

> *Healing begins not as retreat, but as restoration—the recalibration of how you understand your own experience within a system that wasn't built for you.*

WHY HEALING HAS TO BE NAMED

Teacher education programs are not built to account for the cumulative weight of being misread, under-mentored, or positioned outside the intellectual center of a curriculum that claims to prepare you.

Strategic silence can begin to feel like uncertainty. Careful calibration can start to resemble self-doubt. Adaptation—the skill that allowed you to navigate—can begin to blur into compromise.

Healing begins when those distortions are named. When experiences are examined rather than simply absorbed, they can be situated within broader patterns. What felt personal becomes interpretable as structural. That shift restores clarity. It rebuilds trust in your own judgment.

REAL TALK

The reframe that changes everything: you were not struggling because you lacked what it takes. You were navigating systems that required more from you than they required from everyone else. That is not a personal failing. It is a structural reality. Naming it correctly is the beginning of understanding your own experience accurately.

HOPE AS PRACTICE

Hope, through this process, evolves.

Early in the journey, it is often tied to expectation. That institutions will eventually see what you bring. That recognition will naturally follow effort. Over time, that version of hope becomes fragile. It depends too much on external validation.

What replaces it is more durable. Hope grounded in commitment to students, in connection to community, and in a purpose that extends beyond any single institution. This version of hope shows up in classrooms where students feel seen. Where teaching becomes more than instruction. Where a young person understands, perhaps for the first time, what is possible for someone who looks like them.

Hope becomes practice.

RECLAMATION

Reclaiming the profession is not about gaining access to something newly available.

It is about recognizing a lineage that has always existed. Cultural insight, relational depth, and interpretive awareness are not supplemental to teaching. They are central to it. Reclamation affirms that truth.

From that recognition, professional posture shifts. Presence becomes expansive rather than conditional. Leadership emerges through clarity, consistency, and purpose. The classroom becomes not just a place of instruction but of affirmation and intellectual development.

Reclamation is not a retreat from challenge. It is the point at which endurance begins to translate into authorship.

Healing, hope, and reclamation are not endpoints. They are foundations. And from that place, the profession is not simply entered.

It is redefined.

PLAYBOOK MOVE

- Audit your professional narrative. How have you been describing your experience to yourself? Rewrite it with precision—one that reflects your capability accurately, not institutional framing.
- Identify one moment from your training that reflects your teaching at its best—where you taught with full authority and full presence. Return to that moment when the institutional noise gets loud. It is evidence.
- Engage with the intellectual traditions that ground your practice. Let their frameworks reinforce what you already know.
- When healing feels abstract, make it concrete. Interpret one piece of feedback this week through a structural lens rather than a personal one. Notice what changes.

CHAPTER 15

The Calling: Why Black Men Stay

After healing comes a quieter, more deliberate question.

Why stay?

If the journey through teacher education has required sustained awareness, strategy, and effort within systems that don't always fully reflect your experience—what calls Black men to remain?

The answer is not rooted in denial. It is grounded in something more durable than comfort: the recognition that the impact of presence is too consequential to walk away from without serious reflection.

> *Presence changes environments. That is not symbolic. It is consequential.*

WHAT STAYING LOOKS LIKE IN PRACTICE

For most Black men, the calling doesn't arrive as a single moment of certainty.

It develops through ordinary interactions that carry unexpected weight. A student's confidence shifts because someone finally sees him clearly. A young person recognizes that intellectual authority can look like him. A classroom becomes a space where expectations are high, dignity is preserved, and authority is grounded in care rather than control.

Young people absorb models long before they develop the language to describe them. They internalize what leadership looks like, what scholarship feels like, and what integrity requires. When those models are limited, imagination narrows. When they are expanded, new possibilities emerge.

Staying becomes less about individual progression and more about collective responsibility.

SCENARIO: WHAT THE STUDENT REMEMBERED

Years after graduating, a former student tracked down his seventh-grade English teacher—a Black man who had since become a department chair—to tell him something. He remembered the day the teacher handed back an essay with extensive comments. Not red corrections—actual engagement with the ideas. He had told the student: "Your argument is original. I want to see you take it further." The student was twelve. He had never had a teacher engage his ideas that way. He went on to study literature in college. He came back to say that the moment had mattered more than the teacher knew.

That conversation took four minutes. Its impact took years to fully surface. This is what staying makes possible.

Lineage and Legacy

Many Black men who remain in teaching were shaped by someone who invested in them without recognition or reward.

Teaching becomes a continuation of that investment. It extends forward what was once given. Staying reflects continuity—ensuring that what has been received is not lost but multiplied.

Black men don't remain because the profession has always affirmed them. They remain while continuing to name what needs to change, advocate for better conditions, and mentor those who follow in ways that make the path clearer.

The calling is not loud. It is steady.

It is the understanding that teaching is not simply a profession. It is a form of stewardship. What is shaped in classrooms today will define the profession for those who come next.

Experience brings clarity. Those who have navigated educational systems develop a refined understanding of how those systems function. They recognize where expectations are explicit and where they are implied. They see where opportunity exists and where it can be strengthened. Over time, this awareness becomes leverage.

With time, presence becomes influence. Those who remain mentor newer educators, contribute to professional conversations, and help shape how teaching is understood and practiced. Their impact extends beyond individual classrooms.

Leaving is understandable. Remaining is consequential.

Presence matters not only for what it offers in the present, but for what it makes possible over time. The absence of Black men from classrooms shapes what students believe is possible. It narrows the range of professional models available at a moment when imagination is still being formed.

The calling is not about the profession recognizing you. It is about you recognizing what your presence makes possible.

That is why staying matters. Not as sacrifice. As strategy. As stewardship.

PLAYBOOK MOVE

- When the institutional demands become heavy, return to the specific impact that anchored your decision to teach. The student. The classroom. The conversation that mattered. That specificity sustains purpose in ways that general motivation cannot.
- Set the terms of your staying. What do you need to remain effective and well? Name those conditions clearly—to yourself, and when appropriate, to those with institutional authority to respond.
- Invest in those who come after you. Mentoring a newer educator is the most direct way to multiply your impact beyond your own classroom.
- Define what calling means for you concretely—not as an abstract value but as a specific orientation toward specific students in a specific community.

CHAPTER 16

A Blueprint for Institutional Redesign: What Teacher Education Must Do Now

The experiences traced throughout this book are not the result of individual shortcomings.

They are the predictable outcomes of systems designed without Black men at the center. The patterns are visible. The analysis is clear. What remains is the institutional decision to act.

> ***What has been designed can be redesigned. The question is whether institutions are willing to do the work.***

COMMUNITY: ENGINEER BELONGING

You already know what this looks like in practice. The group chat. The peer who decoded the supervisor's feedback. The study session that became something more.

That was community. You built it. Now imagine if the institution had built it first.

In most programs, community among Black male candidates exists informally—built through peer networks, group chats, and collective navigation. This informal infrastructure is powerful. It is also evidence of an institutional gap.

Structured cohort models that connect Black male candidates across a program's timeline transform community from an individual coping mechanism into a designed institutional asset. Formalized mentorship systems with trained mentors, defined expectations, and evaluation standards move mentorship from a lucky encounter to a reliable resource.

Scholarships, stipends, paid clinical experiences, fee waivers for licensure exams, and flexible program sequencing are not supplemental amenities. They are the architecture of equitable access. When these structures are absent, the candidates most likely to leave are those the program claims most to want to retain.

Institutions must track movement through the pipeline—not just enrollment at the beginning—and use that data to identify where access breaks down.

REPRESENTATION: FROM PRESENCE TO AUTHORITY

Representation is not about headcounts. It is about who defines what good teaching looks like, who evaluates whether it was achieved, and who sits in the rooms where those decisions get made.

When Black educators are visible in enrollment data but absent from curriculum committees and hiring panels, that is not representation. That is a placeholder.

Meaningful representation requires intentional hiring into positions of authority.

Integration of diverse intellectual traditions into foundational coursework—not elective seminars. Creation of visible leadership pathways that Black men can see and pursue. When Black educators hold authority over how the field defines itself, representation becomes structural rather than symbolic.

EQUITY: ACCOUNTABILITY OVER ASPIRATION

Equity is not a value. It is a practice. And practices can be measured.

Start with one question: What is the completion rate for Black male candidates in your program, and how does it compare to the overall rate? If your institution doesn't track that, that is the answer.

Equity commitments that exist only in mission statements produce no measurable change.

Equity as accountability requires institutions to ask—and answer—difficult questions about persistence rates, progression patterns, and evaluation outcomes, disaggregated by race and gender. When disparities are identified, they must lead to redesign. Not explanation.

Institutional redesign is not a one-time project. It is an ongoing practice of alignment. Programs that treat redesign as a project with a completion date will find themselves back at the beginning after a few years. Programs that build redesign into their regular institutional rhythms create the conditions for cumulative and durable change.

> **REAL TALK**
>
> If you are in a position to advocate for change within your program—as a student representative, through a capstone project, in an exit interview—use this framework. The language of design is more actionable than the language of complaint. Name what is absent. Propose what would work. Build the case with specificity.

THE MEASURE IS IMPLEMENTATION

The question moving forward is not one of awareness.

That foundation has been established. The question is execution—and the measure will be what institutions are actually willing to change.

This is not about extending opportunity as a gesture. It is about strengthening alignment between values and design.

When teacher education is designed for the full range of those entering it, the profession becomes more rigorous in its thinking, more reflective in its practice, and more aligned with the communities it serves.

That is not a concession to diversity. It is an enhancement of educational quality.

PLAYBOOK MOVE

- Know your program's data. Ask about completion rates and licensure outcomes disaggregated by race and gender. If your institution doesn't track it, that is itself important information.
- When advocating for structural change, lead with design proposals rather than grievances. "Here is what is missing and here is what it would look like" is more persuasive than "here is what is wrong."
- The most powerful institutional advocacy is specific and evidence-based. Before any meeting about program concerns, write down three concrete observations and three concrete proposals. Walk in with both.
- Connect with alumni. Those who have graduated can tell you what institutional decisions made a lasting difference.

CHAPTER 17

A Letter to Black Male Educators

To every Black man who has entered teacher education questioning whether he belonged—

who has stood in front of a classroom and wondered if he was enough—

who has moved through institutional spaces aware that he was often interpreted before he was fully understood:

This was written with you in mind.

What has been required of you extends far beyond completing a program or meeting a set of academic benchmarks. You have navigated environments that did not always reflect you fully. You have carried yourself with composure in moments that demanded restraint. You have continued to show up for students while still finding your own footing within the profession.

That is not incidental. It reflects discipline, awareness, and strength shaped through experience.

You are not an exception. You are part of a lineage.

The work you bring into classrooms is layered. It is informed not only by coursework and formal preparation, but by lived experience, community, and memory. It reflects what was learned long before any syllabus. When you enter a classroom, you are not simply delivering content. You are extending a lineage of educators, thinkers, and community builders who shaped this field across generations—often without recognition.

You understand what it means to be misread.

You recognize the subtle shifts that occur when you enter a room. You know the internal calculations that come before speaking, responding, or challenging. You know what it means to be perceived before being fully known.

And still, you teach with depth. You lead with clarity. You remain.

Students feel that difference—even when they cannot name it. They recognize when authority is steady without being harsh, when expectations are high without being diminishing, when correction is grounded in care rather than control. For many of them, your presence expands what they believe is possible.

That impact often goes unspoken. It is not unnoticed.

> ***You are not here by accident. You are here because of your preparation, your capability, your thinking, and your ability to navigate complexity with intention.***

At the same time—the expectations placed on you are often disproportionate. You are asked to mentor, to stabilize, to step into moments others step away from. The weight of that responsibility is real. Naming that does not weaken your commitment. It clarifies it.

You deserve environments that recognize your full contribution. Spaces where you do not have to reduce yourself in order to belong. Systems that evaluate your work with clarity and fairness. Mentorship that invests in your growth rather than depending on your labor. Community that is intentional, sustained, and real.

Your presence matters.

It matters for students still forming their sense of possibility. It matters for future educators searching for models of leadership and integrity. It matters for a profession continuing to evolve toward greater alignment with the communities it serves.

The fact that you remain is not simply a reflection of endurance. It is an expression of purpose.

You are not alone in navigating what this work requires. The isolation that can feel like a personal condition is a structural one—produced by design decisions that did not account for your presence. Naming it correctly makes it legible. And legibility is the beginning of engaging it with intention.

And because you are still here—the future of this work will be shaped by your presence, your perspective, and your continued commitment.

CONCLUSION

Becoming Visible and Rewriting the Profession

Teacher education in the United States has never been a neutral space.

It was shaped within social and racial hierarchies that determined who would teach, whose knowledge would be recognized, and whose presence would feel expected. Black men were rarely centered. When they entered, they were treated as exceptions rather than foundational contributors.

This work began by examining what it means to move through a system shaped in that way. What it ends with is clear: the system itself must evolve.

> ***Black men do not encounter difficulty in teacher education because they lack intelligence, discipline, or commitment. They encounter difficulty because they move through environments not consistently designed with their histories, identities, or cultural knowledge in mind.***

WHAT THIS WORK HAS REVEALED

Black men experience being both highly visible and structurally overlooked.

They navigate misinterpretations of tone, authority, and presence. They carry forms of labor that are rarely named yet consistently required—emotional, cultural, interpretive, strategic. And still, they remain. Not because the system has fully supported them, but because the work of teaching carries a purpose that extends beyond any single institution.

Representation alone cannot repair what structure leaves unaddressed. Access alone cannot sustain what equity fails to stabilize. Visibility alone cannot transform a profession if it remains symbolic. Without intentional community, representation can isolate. Without equity, access can become fragile.

A Different Future—Already in Motion

A different future is both necessary and within reach.

A Black man enters a teacher education program and does not have to search for affirmation or familiarity. He encounters peers, faculty, and leadership that reflect a broader range of experiences. He engages curriculum that treats multiple intellectual traditions as foundational. He participates in conversations that are rigorous, reflective, and grounded.

In that future, belonging is not negotiated. It is embedded.

Elements of this future already exist. There are classrooms grounded in dignity and high expectations. Programs beginning to examine their design with greater honesty. Networks of educators supporting one another across institutions. The question is not whether change is possible. It is whether it will be sustained.

The goal cannot remain survival. Survival was necessary. It cannot define what comes next.

The goal is transformation. A profession where Black men are not seen as anomalies but as integral. Where their scholarship is recognized, their leadership is cultivated, and their contributions are embedded within the structure of teacher education itself.

Not someday. Now.

What this book has documented is not a crisis. It is an opportunity. The patterns are clear. The analysis is grounded. The framework is available. What teacher education now requires is not more diagnosis but more decision—the institutional willingness to act on what is already known.

It lives in classrooms where Black men teach with clarity, lead with integrity, and expand what students believe is possible.

Teacher education does not lack awareness. It lacks the will to act on what it knows with the same urgency it applies to other institutional priorities.

That is the gap this work names. And that is the gap that can close.

WHAT YOU CAN DO NEXT

This book ends. The work does not.

If you are a Black man navigating teacher education: use this book as a map. Name what is structural. Build your network deliberately. Find your mentors. Document what costs you. And when the institution isn't moving, move anyway—with strategy, not just endurance.

If you are a faculty member, program director, or institutional leader: the C.A.R.E. Model is not a reading list. It is a redesign framework. Community. Access. Representation. Equity. Appendix B gives you the baseline audit. Start there. Measure what you find. Change what needs changing.

If you are a researcher, policymaker, or advocate: the patterns documented here are not anecdotal. They are consistent, cross-institutional, and structural. They call for coordinated response, not isolated intervention. Use this work as evidence.

And if you are someone who simply picked up this book because something in the title felt familiar—because you have stood in a room and wondered if you were supposed to be there—then you already know what this book is about. That knowledge is not incidental. It is exactly the kind of insight this field needs most.

Become visible. Build the system that sees you. Leave it better than you found it.

That work is already underway.

ACKNOWLEDGEMENTS

Standing on What Was Built

Writing about Black men across K–12 education and teacher preparation pathways requires first recognizing the generations who made this work possible.

Long before many of us entered classrooms or higher education environments, Black educators, organizers, spiritual leaders, and community anchors created spaces for learning, protection, and growth. Their work was not always visible or formally acknowledged. Yet it shaped the conditions that made this work possible. Their influence lives in everyday acts of teaching, mentoring, correcting, and believing.

This work stands on that foundation.

To the Black male preservice teachers who contributed to this research: you trusted me with moments that institutions often move past too quickly. You shared not only your challenges, but your clarity, discipline, and vision. This book carries your voice. I hope you see yourselves reflected here with the dignity and depth you deserve.

To those who offered guidance, challenge, and affirmation along the way: your influence is present throughout this work. In the moments when direction was not clear, mentorship mattered. To those who recognized potential when systems did not fully respond to it—thank you.

My experiences within advanced study further clarified the patterns explored in this book. I encountered both support and silence. I experienced moments of affirmation and moments that revealed the limits of institutional understanding. Together, those experiences made visible how systems operate in practice. They deepened my analysis and strengthened my commitment.

Behind this work is also family and community. Naming patterns that are often left unspoken carries weight. That work is made possible through patience, encouragement, and steadiness. Thank you for providing grounding when the work became heavy and for reminding me why it mattered.

And finally—this work is for Black men across K–12 and teacher education spaces. These experiences are not isolated and they are not incidental. They reflect a longer lineage of educators, thinkers, and community builders who have shaped this field across generations, often without recognition.

You are not an exception. You are part of that lineage.

Your presence matters. Your perspective matters. Your leadership matters.

FINAL REFLECTION

What This Work Demands of Us

Every book carries a demand.

Not just for the reader. For the institution. For the field. For everyone who operates within systems that shape who teaches, who leads, and whose knowledge is treated as foundational.

This final reflection is not a summary of what has already been said. It is a direct statement of what this work requires of the people and institutions that encounter it.

This work has examined what it means to occupy space as the only one in the room and still contribute with intention. It has named the strain of being interpreted before being understood. It has examined the misreading of confidence, the narrowing of professional identity, and the often-unseen labor required to construct belonging within environments where it was not structurally ensured.

In doing so, it reframes resilience. Not as an inherent trait. Not as individual toughness. But as disciplined adaptation to conditions that require more than they should.

Black men are not deficits within teacher education. They are contributors whose presence strengthens the profession. They expand classrooms by expanding imagination. They bring relational awareness, cultural knowledge, and pedagogical clarity that deepen the work of teaching.

What this work calls for is not admiration. It is responsibility.

Community cannot remain informal or dependent on individual effort. Access cannot depend on personal sacrifice. Representation cannot remain symbolic without influence. Equity cannot exist as language without practice. These are not abstract values. They are design choices. And design can be improved.

Institutions must continue moving from awareness into sustained action. That work includes transparency in outcomes, intentional investment, and ongoing examination of professional norms. Faculty, administrators, policymakers, and practitioners must consider the assumptions that shape their decisions—including whether evaluation frameworks function equitably in practice, and whether belonging is treated as something to be earned or as something to be designed.

The patterns are visible. The insights are established. The direction is clear.

What remains is consistency.

Teacher education now faces a defining choice: continue relying on individual resilience, or strengthen the conditions that make success more sustainable. That choice will shape not only who enters the profession, but how the profession evolves.

The work has been named. The responsibility is shared. What happens next will reflect the extent to which that responsibility is carried forward with intention and action.

APPENDIX A

Preservice Leadership Framework

A Foundational Orientation for Black Male Educators

The Preservice Leadership Framework provides structural orientation for Black men navigating teacher education and early entry into K–12 practice. It is designed to stabilize professional identity, reduce interpretive ambiguity, and strengthen positioning within complex institutional environments.

Identity Anchoring	Professional stability begins with interpretive clarity. This domain helps distinguish between structural tension and perceived personal inadequacy, centering reflection on the conditions that affirm intellectual authority. As these patterns are named with precision, professional posture stabilizes.
Network Deliberation	Thriving requires the intentional construction of professional ecosystems: intellectual mentorship, peer accountability, cultural affirmation, and institutional navigation. This domain moves support from informal to strategic and sustained.
Strategic Agency	Teacher education operates through both visible standards and invisible codes. Strategic Agency develops the institutional fluency to navigate both—aligning communication, clarifying expectations, documenting practice, and responding to ambiguity through inquiry rather than internalization.

Boundary Stewardship	Black male educators are frequently positioned as stabilizers or disciplinarians before being recognized as scholars. This domain provides structure for defining and protecting professional scope without sacrificing relational capacity.

Together, these domains form a foundation for navigating teacher education with clarity, intention, and strategic positioning. What begins as a framework for navigation evolves into a structure for influence.

APPENDIX B

Institutional Redesign Baseline

A Structural Equity Orientation Framework

Meaningful equity reform in teacher education requires architectural review. The six domains below constitute the baseline for that examination. They function as an integrated system: when implemented collectively, they move equity from aspiration to structure.

Pipeline Stability	Examine faculty and leadership demographics alongside recruitment, retention, progression, and completion patterns for Black male candidates. Equity requires a longitudinal view of how individuals move through systems and where breakdowns occur.
Structured Belonging	Move mentorship and community from informal practice into institutional infrastructure. Mentorship must include defined roles, trained mentors, evaluation standards, and consistent access points—recognized as institutional labor, not voluntary goodwill.
Curricular Legitimacy	Conduct systematic curricular reviews assessing whose scholarship anchors the intellectual core of the program. Racial and cultural analysis must be embedded across foundational coursework as central, not supplemental.

Financial Access	Address the material conditions shaping persistence: unpaid clinical placements, certification exam costs, inflexible structures. Align financial resources with equity goals through scholarships, stipends, paid clinical experiences, and exam support.
Interpretive Equity	Implement bias recognition training, establish standardized evaluative language, and create structured review processes for contested assessments. Without calibration, evaluation can reproduce inequity under the appearance of objectivity.
Leadership Continuity	Build structured pathways into faculty roles, program leadership, and governance. These pathways must be visible, resourced, and supported through mentorship and sponsorship. Without structure, leadership advancement remains inconsistent.

These domains are not a final solution. They are a structural baseline.

The patterns are clear. The direction is defined. What remains is sustained implementation.

Becoming Visible: How Black Men Navigate, Resist, and Transform Teacher Education

Dr. William A. Anders · ENLA Solutions Group, LLC · 2026

ABOUT THE AUTHOR

Dr. William A. Anders

Dr. William A. Anders is a scholar-practitioner and nationally recognized voice in educator pipeline development.

He specializes in the design and sustainability of pathways into the teaching profession for Black and Brown men. His scholarship focuses on how educational systems can move beyond access toward sustained belonging, representation, and measurable impact.

Across higher education institutions and K–12 systems, Dr. Anders has contributed to large-scale efforts to strengthen educator pathways through cross-sector collaboration, structured mentorship, and data-informed design.

His research is grounded in Critical Race Theory, Critical University Studies, and phenomenological inquiry. It examines how Black male preservice teachers navigate institutional environments and how those environments can be structurally redesigned to support their development, recognition, and long-term success. His work bridges lived experience with systems-level analysis, offering both critique and actionable direction for institutional redesign.

He is the architect of the C.A.R.E. Model—Community, Access, Representation, and Equity—a framework that emerged directly from his research. Through his writing, speaking, and consulting, Dr. Anders advances the development of systems that recognize and sustain the talent already present in their classrooms.

For speaking, consulting, or scholarly collaboration:

www.DrWilliamAnders.com

www.ingramcontent.com/pod-product-compliance
Lightning Source LLC
LaVergne TN
LVHW010937110826
845149LV00013B/2648
* 9 7 9 8 9 9 5 6 2 8 9 1 0 *